Hull Libraries

1 1 DEC 2013

0 5 AUG 2023

0 3 FEB 2014

0 7 APR 2014

1 3 NOV 2014

1 2 DEC 2014

1 7 FEB 2015

2 7 MAY 2017

3 1 JAN 2022

Please return/renew this item by the due date.
Items may be renewed at any library, by phone or online.

Tel: 01482 210000

www.hullcc.gov.uk

HULL LIBRARIES

To watch some great street sport videos, scan the QR codes with your smartphone. See pages 9, 11, 15, 17 and 21.

First published in 2013 by
Franklin Watts
338 Euston Road
London NW1 3BH

Franklin Watts Australia
Level 17/207 Kent Street
Sydney NSW 2000

Copyright © Franklin Watts 2013
All rights reserved.
Series editor: Adrian Cole

Packaged for Franklin Watts by Storeybooks
rita@storeybooks.co.uk
Designer: Rita Storey

A CIP catalogue record for this book is available from the British Library.

Printed in China

Dewey classification: 796

ISBN
(HB): 978 1 4451 1947 2
(Library ebook): 978 1 4451 2587 9

Franklin Watts is a division of Hachette Children's Books, an Hachette UK company
www.hachette.co.uk

Photo acknowledgements

B.Stefanov/Shutterstock.com: 20. homydesign/Shutterstock.com: 9. LatinContent/Getty Images: 8. Parkour Generation: 4b and 17 (Shirley Darlington). pio3/Shutterstock.com: 18 – 19. Shutterstock: 3, 6, 7, 10, 14 – 15 and 16. Team extreme: 1, 4t, 5, 11, 12, 13 and 21.

Every attempt has been made to clear copyright. Should there be any inadvertent omission, please apply to the Publishers for rectification.

Contents

Street Sport 4

Skateboarding 6

Street BMX 10

Scooters 13

Parkour 14

Streetball 18

Street Skating 20

Street Soccer 22

Glossary 23

Index and Websites 24

Street Sport

A street sport is probably happening on a street or in a skatepark near you.

Anyone can take part in street sport.

"Street sports are awesome."

There are fewer rules in street sports than in other sports.

Skateboarding

Skateboarding is a fast and exciting street sport.

Karen Jonz
Karen Jonz of Brazil has twice been World Skateboarding Champion.

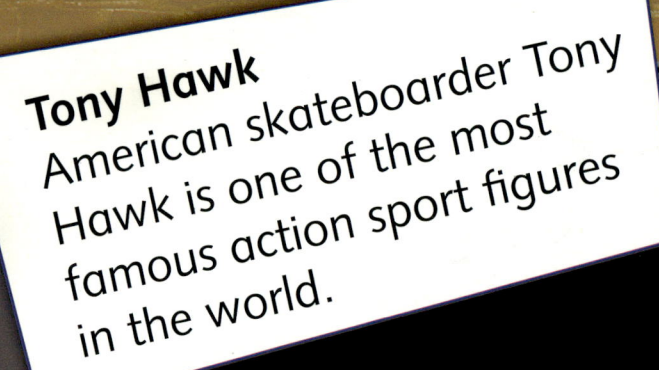

Tony Hawk
American skateboarder Tony Hawk is one of the most famous action sport figures in the world.

In 1999 Tony was the first skateboarder to land a 900, one of the most difficult skateboard moves.

"It feels like you are at one with the board."

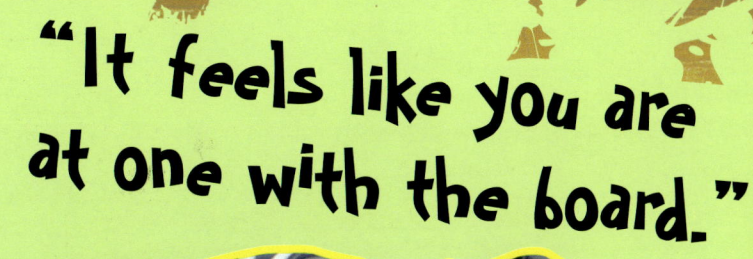

Downhill skateboarding can be dangerous.

Downhill skateboarding has its own competitions.

Street BMX

BMX riders that do tricks and grinds are called freestyle riders.

"You have to commit to every trick. If you do you're a winner."

Flatland BMX riders do tricks on flat areas such as car parks.

Kyle Blake
Some very good BMX riders, like Kyle Blake, can earn money doing stunt shows and exhibitions.

Scooters

Scooters can be used to do jumps, spins and tricks.

Scooter riders can do both BMX and skateboard tricks.

Parkour

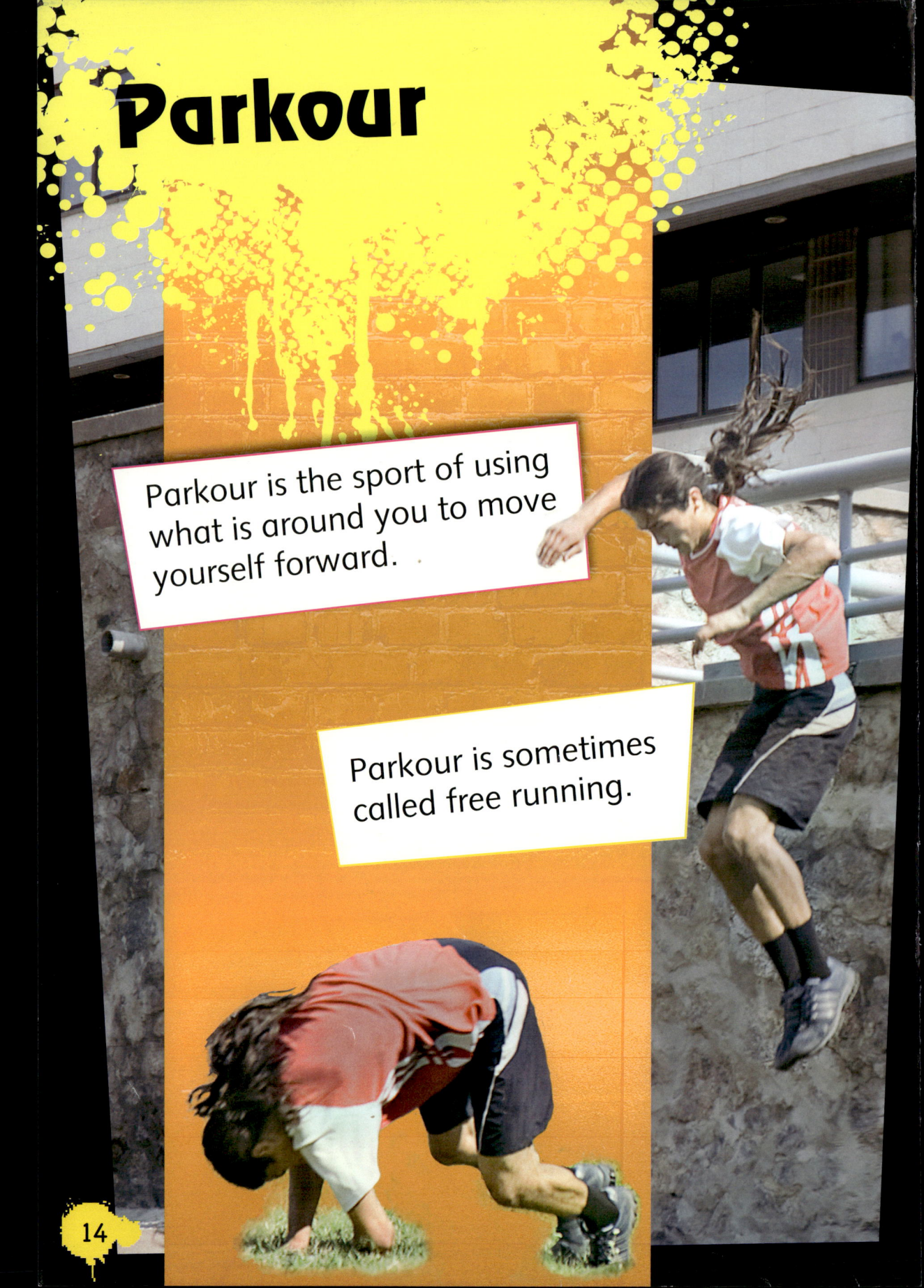

Parkour is the sport of using what is around you to move yourself forward.

Parkour is sometimes called free running.

Parkour is not a competition. Each person can make up their own course.

When parkour is done well it looks easy.

"Parkour makes me feel totally alive."

To do parkour well takes concentration, fitness, balance and a lot of training.

Buildings, rails and walls are used to help the runner move forward.

Shirley Darlington
Shirley did gymnastics and ballet before taking up parkour.

17

Streetball

Streetball is a type of basketball played on street courts.

There are fewer rules in streetball than in basketball.

Streetball players have their own style.

The number of players in a streetball team is not always the same.

Street Skating

Freestyle skaters use inline skates. They can do jumps, grinds and balances.

Freestyle skaters can reach very high speeds.

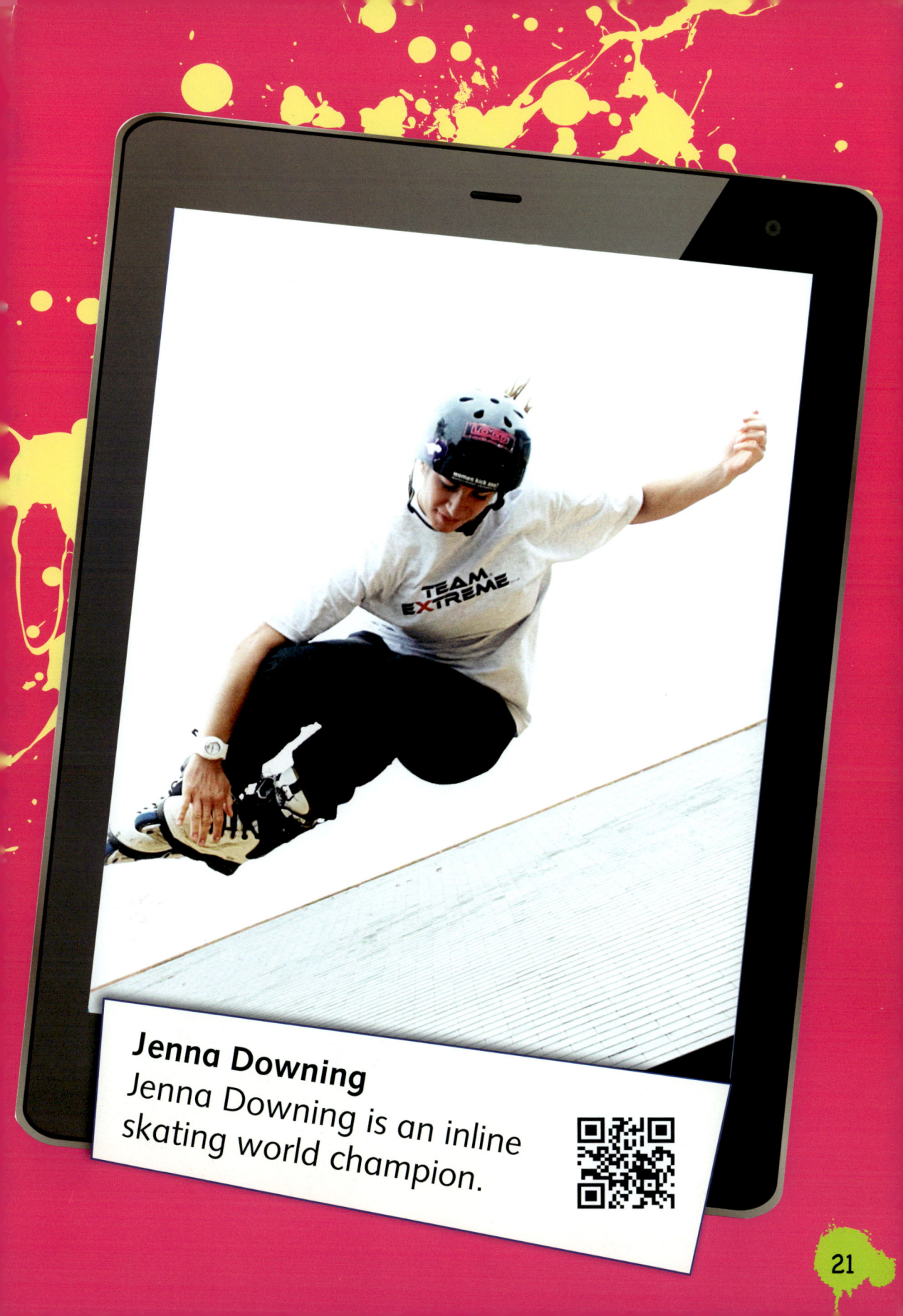

Jenna Downing
Jenna Downing is an inline skating world champion.

Street Soccer

Street soccer is played in streets, parks and gardens all over the world. The rules can be changed to fit the number of players.

Street soccer has its own competitions.

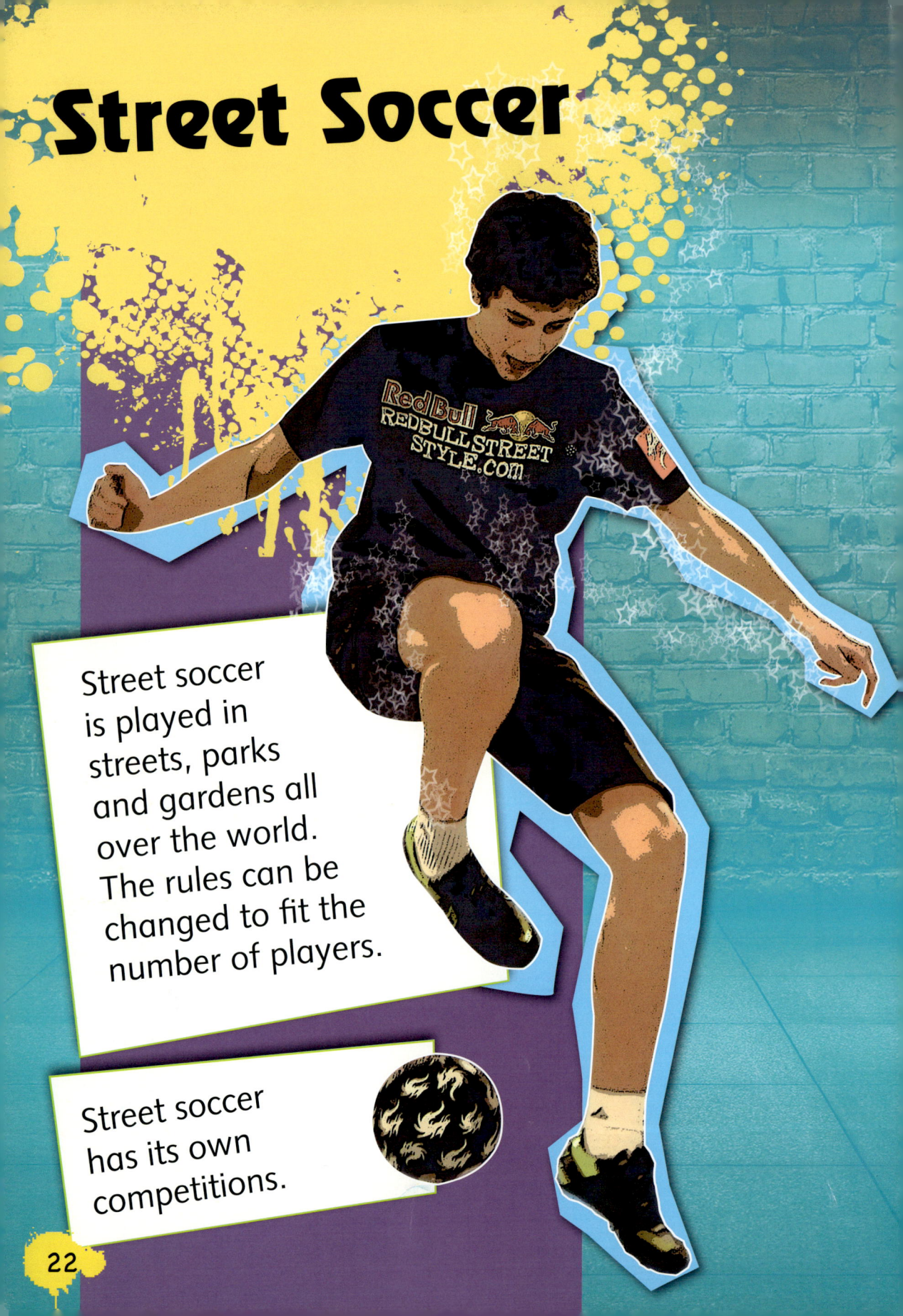

Glossary

A 900 A two and a half spin in the air performed off a skateboard ramp.

Basketball A game played by two teams. The object is to score goals by throwing a ball through one of the hoops fixed at each end of the court.

BMX A type of bicycle used for racing and stunt riding.

Flatland A type of BMX done on flat areas such as car parks.

Free running The sport of using what is around you to move yourself forward. Also called parkour.

Inline skates Skates with four or five wheels arranged in a line. Also called rollerblades.

Parkour The sport of using what is around you to move yourself forward. Also called free running.

Scooters A low footboard between two wheels controlled by an upright steering handle attached at the front. Scooters are used in street sport to perform jumps, spins and tricks.

Skateboard A narrow piece of wood on four wheels used by skateboarders to perform jumps and tricks.

Skateboarding A fast and exciting street sport performed on a skateboard.

Skatepark An area set aside for skateboarding and other street sports.

Streetball A type of basketball played on street courts.

Street soccer A type of soccer played in streets, parks and gardens.

To watch some great street sport in action, scan the QR codes on these pages or copy the links below into your browser.

9   http://www.youtube.com/watch?v=SLyG0mUnw4A
11 http://www.videojug.com/film/how-to-do-tricks-on-a-bmx-bike
15 http://www.youtube.com/watch?v=WKJPorL4ZqA
17 http://www.youtube.com/watch?v=TXPNd7jqQkg
21 http://vimeo.com/11472040

23

Index

900 8

Ballet 17
Basketball 18
BMX 10, 11, 12, 13

Flatland 11
Free running 14
Freestyle 10, 20

Grinds 10, 20
Gymnastics 17

Inline skates 20, 21

Jenna Downing 21

Karen Jonz 7
Kyle Blake 12

Parkour 14, 15, 16, 17

Scooters 13
Shirley Darlington 17
Skateboard 8, 13
Skateboarders 8
Skateboarding 6, 7, 9
Skatepark 4, 20
Skaters 20

Spins 13
Streetball 18, 19
Street BMX 10
Street courts 18
Street skating 20
Street soccer 22
Street sport 4, 5, 6

Tony Hawk 8
Tricks 10, 11, 13

Websites

www.parkouruk.org
Information on the art of Parkour.
The site for the national governing body of parkour/freerunnning in the UK.

www.parkourgenerations.com/
A site full of exciting information videos and lots more about parkour.

www.teamextreme.co.uk/
Check out the teamextreme BMX, skateboaders, inline skaters, skateboarders and scooter riders. Watch tricks and how-to's by clicking on the links.

Please note: every effort has been made by the Publishers to ensure that the websites in this book contain no inappropriate or offensive material. However, because of the nature of the Internet, it is impossible to guarantee that the contents of these sites will not be altered. We strongly advise that Internet access is supervised by a responsible adult.